A souvenir guide

Powis Castle
Powys

National Trust

Welcome to Powis

Welcome to *Castell Coch* (the Red Castle), as it is called in Welsh. In the 13th century, a Prince of Powys chose these stones to replace the wood which a Prince of Gwynedd burned down — it is a Welsh Castle built by a Welsh Prince who stood between the marauding of Gwynedd and the acquisitive English. Here Hawise the Hardy held out against her uncle, who had determined to take the castle and lands from her, and the King of England affirmed her claim in recognition of her persistence and courage. The Lollard Sir John Oldcastle (Shakespeare's Falstaff) was brought here, before being taken to London and handed over to the Bishops, to whom his 'friend' Henry V betrayed him; once there he was hanged, drawn and quartered, merely because he believed that people should be able to read the Bible in their native language.

The Herberts, originating from Abergavenny, bought Powis in the 1580s, when the last of the Lords of Powis died out. Everything looked above-board, but Sir Edward Herbert who bought the castle was conveniently 'connected' — his cousin John Herbert of Swansea was married to Jane Orwell who just happened to be mistress to the last Lord of Powis.

The family has been here ever since, despite a tendency to side with the wrong camp, in the Civil War and then with King James II whom they served in exile. In 1952, George Powis the 4th Earl (3rd creation) decided to give his beloved castle and gardens to the nation — the transfer to the National Trust happened on his death bed, which was also curiously the year I was born. Fifty years before, he and his wife Violet undertook a comprehensive restoration of the castle and grounds with the tasteful help of the architect G. F. Bodley. As you go round it you will see much of their labour of love and considerable expense. It is a beautiful building in a beautiful setting to be admired and enjoyed, but I hope too you will sense its connection with that turbulence of native princes and the English, and with all the history since, which this survivor still stands for.

John Herbert
(8th Earl of Powis)

Left The medieval drum towers of Powis Castle, with the statue of *Fame* by Andries Carpentiere, *c*.1705, in the foreground

Medieval Powis

Powis Castle was built in the mid-13th century by a Welsh ruler, Gruffudd ap Gwenwynwyn, lord of Powys. He wanted to establish his independence from the aggressive princes of Gwynedd (North Wales) who were traditional enemies. In contrast, the castles of North Wales (such as Caernarfon, Harlech and Conwy) were built by the English to consolidate Edward I's conquest.

By the late 13th century, Llywelyn ap Gruffudd of Gwynedd had established himself as Prince of Wales, and in 1274 he destroyed Powis Castle and forced Gruffudd ap Gwenwynwyn into exile. However, within three years, Llywelyn's principality crumbled and Gruffudd of Powys was able to regain his lordship and rebuild Powis Castle.

Gruffudd, his son and grandson all died by 1309, and with no male heir, the castle and lordship passed to an heiress, Hawise, who married Sir John Charlton from Shropshire. In 1312, Hawise's uncle, Gruffudd Fychan, attacked the castle in an attempt to claim the lordship. Charlton repaired the castle and built the great drum towers that you can still see today.

Descendants of the Charltons continued as Lords of Powis for over 100 years. In 1421 the lack of a male heir resulted in the castle and estate being divided between two daughters, Joyce and Joan, who had married Sir John Grey and Sir John Tiptoft respectively. Under the Tiptofts and their successor, Lord Dudley, the Outer Ward of the castle became neglected. In the 1530s Edward Grey, Lord Powis, took possession of the whole castle and began a major rebuilding programme that made Powis the most imposing noble residence in North and Central Wales.

In 1578, the last of the Greys leased Powis to Sir Edward Herbert, second son of the 1st Earl of Pembroke.

Dr David Stephenson

Powis Castle: A timeline

Mid-13th century
Powis Castle built by Gruffudd ap Gwenwynwyn, Lord of Powys

1274
Conflict between Llywelyn from Gwynedd and Gruffudd of Powys resulted in the castle being burned and dismantled

1277
Edward I of England attacked Llywelyn; Gruffudd regained Powis. His son Owain started rebuilding, but died in 1293

1309
Owain's son died, leaving no male heir. Lordship passed to Owain's daughter, Hawise, who married Sir John Charlton

1421
Lack of a Charlton male heir resulted in castle and estate being split between two daughters and their husbands (Greys and Tiptofts)

1530s
Edward Grey took over control of whole castle, and began significant rebuilding

1578
Sir Edward Herbert leased Powis Castle. In 1587 he bought the castle outright and began making improvements, notably the Long Gallery

1595
Sir Edward's son William inherited Powis

1629
William Herbert made Lord Powis by Charles I

1651
As a royalist, Percy Herbert, the son of Lord Powis, was convicted of treason by Parliament under Cromwell and imprisoned

1656
Percy inherited Powis when released from prison

1667
Percy's son William inherited Powis and began improvements to the castle

1674
William created Earl by Charles II

1678
William falsely accused by Titus Oates of conspiring against the king, and imprisoned in Tower of London for five years

1687
William created Marquess by James II; 1688 he accompanied James into exile

1696
1st Marquess died still in exile, and title and estate passed to his son William

1703
2nd Marquess and his family returned to reclaim Powis, continued improvements to the castle and garden started by his father

1720s
2nd Marquess's daughter Mary lost family fortune through investments in the French stock market which collapsed; Marquess imprisoned in France for debts

1745
Death of 2nd Marquess; Powis passed to his son, William, who never married

1200s–1629   *1651–1678*   *1687–1745*

1748
3rd Marquess died, leaving Powis to his distant relative Henry Arthur Herbert, rather than his closest Catholic relation, Barbara Herbert

1751
Henry Arthur Herbert married Barbara Herbert; both lost money and increased debts. George II recreated title Earl of Powis for Henry

1772
Henry, 1st Earl (2nd creation) died, leaving Powis to his son George

1801
George, 2nd Earl died unmarried, leaving debts of £177,000 and Powis estates to his nephew Edward Clive on condition he changed his surname to Herbert on his coming of age

1804
Edward Clive (son of Clive of India and brother-in-law to 2nd Earl) granted the title 1st Earl of Powis (3rd creation) by George III. He managed the Powis estates until his son Edward came of age and inherited Powis in 1807

Images left to right

Sir Percy Herbert, 2nd Lord Powis by Paul van Somer

William, 3rd Marquess of Powis as a boy, French, early 18th century

Edward Clive, 1st Earl of Powis by Hugh Douglas Hamilton

Edward (Clive) Herbert, 2nd Earl of Powis by Sir Francis Grant

Violet Powis by John Singer Sargent

1848
Edward Herbert, 2nd Earl, died after a shooting accident, leaving estate to his son, Edward

1891
3rd Earl died unmarried, leaving Powis to his nephew George

1890s–1900s
The 4th Earl and his wife, Violet, restored the castle and gardens

1952
The 4th Earl died, leaving Powis to the National Trust

1748–1804   *1848–1952*

Family highlights

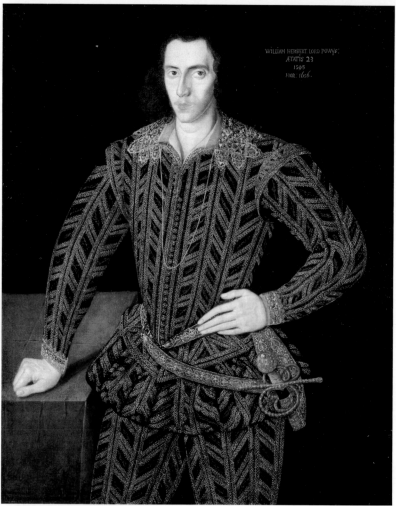

Sir Edward Herbert

In 1578, Powis was leased to Sir Edward Herbert (c.1542–95), the second son of William Herbert, 1st Earl of Pembroke and Anne Parr (sister of Catherine Parr, the sixth wife of Henry VIII). As a second son, Edward had to make his own way in the world. In 1587, he purchased the castle and the estate outright. Edward immediately began making improvements to the castle, but all that still remains is the beautiful Long Gallery dated 1593, with its elaborate plasterwork frieze.

William, 1st Lord Powis

Sir Edward's son William (1574–1656) inherited Powis at the age of 21 and married Lady Eleanor Percy. William was created 1st Lord Powis by Charles I in 1629, and remained loyal to the king during the Civil War. In October 1644, the castle was captured at night by Parliamentary troops. Lord Powis (then aged 70) was taken prisoner and his estates were confiscated. He was initially imprisoned locally, but was later held in the Tower of London, living on an allowance of £4 per week. He died in 1656, never regaining his estates.

Above *William Herbert, 1st Lord Powis*, 1595

Left *Eleanor Percy, Lady Powis*, 1595

William, 1st Marquess

William (*c.*1626–96) was the grandson of the 1st Lord Powis. He was rewarded for his loyalty to the king with titles and high-ranking posts, but also experienced periods of imprisonment and exile as a result of his Catholic faith. During the 1660s, he initiated improvements to the interior (including the Grand Staircase and State Apartment), transforming it from a medieval castle into a mansion fit for a nobleman. William was created an Earl by Charles II in 1674, but in 1678 was falsely accused by Titus Oates of being a conspirator in the 'Popish Plot' to kill the king and replace him with his Catholic younger brother, James. Although the accusations were untrue, the Earl was imprisoned in the Tower of London for five years. In 1685 Charles II died and his brother James became king – an unpopular monarch resented by the Protestant majority. The Earl became a member of the Privy Council, and was made a Marquess by the King in 1687. Together with his wife Elizabeth and their children, William accompanied James II into exile in France in 1688.

William, 2nd Marquess

William (*c.*1665–1745) inherited his father's title in 1696, but remained in exile until he returned to Powis in 1703. The 2nd Marquess continued to make improvements to the castle by commissioning murals, painted ceilings and the Marquess Gates to the east entrance of the castle. He also completed the terraced gardens that his father had started. But the family's fortune was largely destroyed by one of William's daughters, Lady Mary Herbert. As a result of her speculation on the French stock market, by May 1720 she had accumulated a fortune of 6.5 million *livres*, which was all lost when the investments failed. The Marquess was liable for debts equivalent to £170,000, and had to be imprisoned in a Paris jail to avoid his creditors. In 1725 the Marquess was forced to consolidate his debts by re-mortgaging his estates.

Family highlights, continued

Left *George Herbert, 2nd Earl of Powis* by Pompeo Batoni, 1776

Far left *Henry Arthur Herbert, 1st Earl of Powis*, attributed to Thomas Hudson, *c.*1740

Henry Arthur Herbert, 1st Earl (2nd creation)

Lord Herbert of Chirbury (1703–72) lived at Oakly Park, near Ludlow in Shropshire and inherited Powis in 1748 when the 3rd Marquess died without an heir. He persuaded George II to recreate the title of Earl of Powis for him in 1748, and so became the 1st Earl (2nd creation). However, there were rumours that Barbara Herbert's guardian (Lord Montague) was

going to challenge Henry's inheritance of Powis, on the grounds that the 3rd Marquess was drunk when he made his will. Henry countered this by marrying his distant relative Barbara (then aged 16) in 1751.

Both were extravagant in different ways: she was a compulsive gambler and he had spent £20,000 to become an MP. In an effort to settle their debts, in 1771 the Earl sold Oakly Park to his friend Robert Clive, establishing the first link between the Clive family and Powis.

George, 2nd Earl

Henry's son George (1755–1801) inherited Powis in 1772 at the age of 17 and approved the proposal for a new ballroom wing to the castle. He set out on a Grand Tour of Italy, and returned to celebrate his coming of age in the new ballroom in 1776. Subsequently, he spent much of his time (and money) in London. He never married, and on his death in 1801 left debts of £177,000 and the Powis estate to his nephew, Edward Clive, on condition that he changed his surname from Clive to Herbert when he came of age.

Edward Clive, 2nd Lord Clive, 1st Earl of Powis (3rd creation)

Edward Clive (1754–1839) was the son of Robert Clive, who had risen to prominence through his successful military campaigns in India. Edward's marriage to Lady Henrietta Herbert in 1784 had provided financial security for Powis through the Clive family fortune. In 1798, Edward took up the post of Governor of Madras, and was immediately involved in the preparations for war with Tipu Sultan, which resulted in the British victory at Seringapatam in May 1799.

Lord Clive returned to Britain in 1804 and was granted the title of 1st Earl of Powis (3rd creation) partly as a reward for his role in India, but also in recognition of his son's inheritance of Powis Castle from his uncle. He managed the Powis estate until his son (also named Edward) came of age.

George Herbert, 4th Earl of Powis

George (1862–1952) was the great-grandson of Edward Clive, and inherited Powis in 1891. Together he and his wife, Violet, focused on restoring the castle and garden. The 4th Earl suffered three family tragedies: his elder son Percy was fatally wounded on the Somme in 1916; his wife died in 1929 after a car accident; and his younger son Mervyn was killed in an aeroplane crash in 1942 during active service. The Earl died in 1952, and bequeathed Powis Castle to the National Trust.

Below left *Edward Clive, 1st Earl of Powis* by Gervase Spencer

Below right *George Herbert, 4th Earl of Powis* by Sir William Llewellyn

Tour of the House

A superb collection of treasures awaits you at Powis. Exceptional art, statues, furniture and textiles from Europe, India and the Orient adorn the Castle to magnificent effect.

A stately welcome

The Entrance Hall and Grand Staircase were redeveloped by the Herbert family in the late 17th century to reflect their increasing wealth and importance. In 1674, the owner of Powis Castle, William Herbert, 3rd Lord Powis was made an Earl and in 1687 he was created a Marquess. He therefore wanted a fine entrance hall to impress visitors and indicate his status.

The Entrance Hall

The Entrance Hall was an important space, the first of a sequence of rooms collectively known as the State Apartment, a concept first introduced by the French royal court in the 17th century, which involved a series of rooms each more impressive than the previous one. From the Hall, important guests would be invited to climb the Grand Staircase and discover the increasing grandeur and opulence of the state rooms on the first floor.

The Grand Staircase

The Grand Staircase was constructed between 1674 and 1687 by William Winde. The stair treads are made of walnut wood inlaid with sycamore, holly and yew; the banisters include pineapples, which were symbols of hospitality at that time.

Left **The Grand Staircase and Entrance Hall**

Ceiling and wall paintings

The walls and lower ceiling are by Gerard Lanscroon and date from 1705. They are painted in shades of grey to imitate three-dimensional sculpture, a technique known as *grisaille*. Lanscroon also produced the impressive murals both sides of the staircase.

The Smoking Room

Like many other rooms in the castle, this one has been used for different purposes. In 1902, it became a Smoking Room, where gentlemen could retire after dinner to enjoy a cigar, a brandy and perhaps a game of cards, and maybe also discuss business. The door to the right of the fireplace leads to a small washroom where the men could freshen up before rejoining the ladies.

Furniture

To the left of the room is a simple, solid chair dating from the reign of Charles I, which contrasts with some of the more elaborate pieces produced later in the 17th century. The Louis XIV bureau Mazarin under the portrait of Old Parr is a style that was popular in the 1670s. The walnut-veneered longcase clock to the right of the room was made *c.*1680 by Thomas Tompion, the father of British clockmaking.

Above The Smoking Room

Left Walnut-veneered longcase clock *c.*1680 in the Smoking Room

Grand old age

This is a portrait of 'Old Parr', a local hero. He was a Shropshire farm labourer, who was reputedly born in 1483, and lived on a simple diet of buttermilk, bread, onions and green cheese. He became an object of curiosity and in 1635 was taken to London to meet King Charles I who treated him to lavish parties with indulgent food and alcohol. Apparently, the change of lifestyle and diet did not suit him, as he died two weeks later, reputedly aged 152!

The State Dining Room

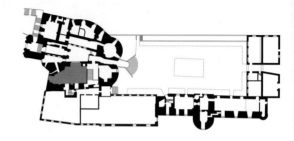

Edwardian makeover

The State Dining Room was probably the original medieval Great Hall, but its use changed over the years. In 1902–4 it was transformed to its present style by the architect G. F. Bodley, as George, the 4th Earl of Powis, felt that a richly decorated Jacobean style was more appropriate for an ancient castle.

Bodley introduced wood panelling on the walls (copied from fragments found in the room) and an elaborate plasterwork ceiling, which was based on the ceiling of the old Reindeer Inn at Banbury. You can still see some original 16th-century plasterwork in the small window alcove. The two oak chimneypieces are decorated with the arms of Lord Powis and his wife, Violet, 16th Baroness Darcy de Knayth. These were both based on Jacobean designs that the 4th Earl greatly admired in the Victoria and Albert Museum.

Family portraits

Several important portraits are displayed in this room. On the far right-hand side you can see portraits of William Herbert, 1st Lord Powis (1574–1656) and his wife, Lady Eleanor Percy (1582/3–1650). On the left-hand wall is a large portrait of Lady Henrietta Herbert (1758–1830), who married Edward, 2nd Lord Clive. On the right are portraits of George Herbert, 4th Earl of Powis (1862–1952) and his wife, Violet (1865–1929). The couple initiated major changes at the beginning of the 20th century: the Earl concentrated on transforming the interior of the castle, while Violet focused on the restoration of the gardens. The portrait to the left of the window recess shows the 5th Countess wearing a golden gown made of 18th-century Indian fabric; the gown is displayed in the Clive Museum.

Left The Dining Room table

Right *Lady Henrietta Antonia Herbert* by Sir Joshua Reynolds, 1777

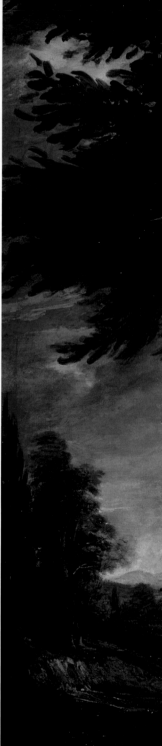

Furniture

The 18th-century dining table and chairs are made of mahogany; the chairs were made *c*.1755 in the style of Thomas Chippendale and still have their original needlework upholstery. There is an unusual horseshoe-shaped table in front of the second fireplace, which was made *c*.1810. It was designed to allow gentlemen to enjoy a few drinks; the small curtain gave some protection from the heat of the fire, and the net was for discarding empty bottles.

Following fashion

Today, we do not see the painting of Lady Henrietta as it was painted by Sir Joshua Reynolds in 1777. A small black-and-white engraving, produced  shortly after the portrait was completed, shows Lady Henrietta with an elaborate hairstyle, but no hat. It seems likely that the original portrait was modified by a different artist when fashions changed.

Above **Horseshoe-shaped wine table, *c*.1810**

The Library

This room was set up as a library in the early 19th century, probably to house the collection of books from Empress Josephine, consort of Napoleon Bonaparte. Many of her books were sold in the 1920s, but some remain in other rooms. In 1841–2 the 2nd Earl added the bookcases and the red and gold embossed wallpaper.

In earlier times this room formed part of the State Apartment created by William Herbert (who later became 1st Marquess of Powis) in the 1660s. It was used as a waiting room between the two more important state rooms adjoining it, now known as the Oak and Blue Drawing Rooms. The blue and gold wooden cornice dates from the 1660s.

Looking up

The ceiling was painted about 1705 by Gerard Lanscroon for the 2nd Marquess, who continued much of the elaborate decoration started by his father. It shows the Marquess's two eldest daughters (Lady Mary and Lady Theresa) seated in the clouds with their younger sisters leaning over the balustrade. The painting depicts Lady Mary as Minerva, Goddess of Wisdom; unfortunately this portrayal was inappropriate, as her financial speculations in the mid-18th century almost ruined the family.

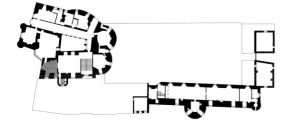

Looking out

The large window provides fine views to the east, looking towards Welshpool. You can also see the great stone stairway leading up to the East Tower, which was the main entrance to the castle until the late 18th century. The ornate gates were made for the 2nd Marquess in 1707.

Fine portraits

The library displays two images of Lord Herbert of Chirbury (1581/3–1648), a distant relative of the Powis Herberts, who lived nearby at Montgomery Castle and was a poet, philosopher and diplomat. A beautiful miniature on vellum, painted by Isaac Oliver about 400 years ago, shows him as a melancholy knight and lover. A bronze bust by Hubert Le Sueur dated 1631 shows Lord Herbert in later life. It is possible Lord Herbert met Le Sueur at the court of Louis XIII, as he was British ambassador to Paris in 1619–24. Lord Herbert's great-great-grandson inherited Powis in 1748. The bust was sold by the family in 1962, but was bought jointly in 1990 by the National Museum of Wales and the National Trust.

Religious items

The Herbert family were Catholics until the mid-18th century, and the collection includes some very fine religious items. The showcase to the left of the fireplace displays an intricately carved boxwood cross which according to family tradition was owned by Mary Queen of Scots; this is possible as research suggests it was made in the 16th century. Underneath is a gold pectoral cross that was presented to Bishop Herbert (1885–1968) when he was Bishop of Kingston.

Opposite above
The Library

Opposite Gerard Lanscroon ceiling painting in the Library

Above Edward Herbert, 1st Lord Herbert of Chirbury by Isaac Oliver

Right Bust of Edward Herbert by Hubert Le Sueur, 1631

The Oak Drawing Room

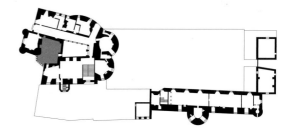

This room has always been the main drawing room, to which the company would retire on important occasions after dining in the Great Chamber (now the Blue Drawing Room). Records show that the ornate decoration introduced by Sir Edward Herbert c.1593, shortly after he purchased the castle in 1587, still existed in 1772. This included wall panelling inlaid with different woods, a chimneypiece supporting busts of Seneca and Aristotle, and the ceiling decorated with the 12 signs of the zodiac.

Some changes were made to the room in the early 19th century, when sash windows were installed. The last major changes were made over a hundred years ago when the 4th Earl employed the architect G. F. Bodley to remodel the interior of several rooms within the castle, with the aim of giving them a more Jacobean style. The large mullioned window, oak panelling and plasterwork ceiling were all installed by Bodley in 1902–4, although you can still see some original Elizabethan plasterwork surrounding the small, high window.

Below The Oak Drawing Room

Delicate veneer
Several 17th-century pieces of furniture feature elaborate marquetry decoration, including the longcase clock to the left of the large window, walnut cabinets and tables. Various woods were used to create the designs, although the green leaves on the cabinet to the right of the alcove are actually made of ivory that has been stained green. This cabinet dates from c.1890 but was made using traditional techniques.

Left *View of Verona from the Ponte Nuovo* by Bernado Bellotto, 1745–7

Below *Edward, 1st Lord Herbert of Chirbury* by an unknown English painter, c.1603–5

Portraits and views

To the left of the fireplace is a portrait of Edward, 1st Lord Herbert of Chirbury, wearing the crimson taffeta robes in which he was created a Knight of the Bath in 1604 by James I.

On the right-hand wall as you enter the room there is a portrait of William, 1st Marquess of Powis. The Marquess and Marchioness were both Catholics, like their ancestors, and were close to James II. While the King was in exile in France, after the Glorious Revolution, he made William a Duke, but this title was never recognised by the English monarchy.

A large portrait of Robert Clive, 1st Lord Clive (1725–74) hangs on the wall opposite the window. His son Edward Clive married Lady Henrietta Herbert in 1784, and became the 1st Earl of Powis (3rd creation). A portrait of Edward as a boy by Thomas Gainsborough, painted c.1763, hangs on the right wall close to the exit.

The View of Verona opposite the fireplace was painted c.1745 by Bernardo Bellotto, who was a nephew and pupil of Canaletto. The painting was bought for Powis in 1981 with the aid of the National Heritage Memorial Fund, National Art Collections Fund, Victoria and Albert Museum Grant-in-Aid scheme and private contributions.

The Gateway Room

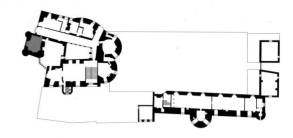

Family portraits

To the right of the window recess is a portrait of Percy, 2nd Lord Powis (c.1598–1667). To the left of the window hangs a portrait of a lady in a beautiful dress, which for many years was thought to show Lady Elizabeth Craven, wife of Percy. However recent research suggests that it may be Lady Elizabeth Somerset, 1st Marchioness of Powis, at a very young age, wearing a dress in the style of an earlier period (that is, Percy's daughter-in-law, rather than his wife).

Left The Gateway Room

Below Lady Elizabeth Somerset, later Marchioness of Powis, c.1650s

This room is named after its position above the eastern gateway, which was the main entrance to the castle until the late 18th century. It has been used at different times as a bedroom and a private sitting room for two Countesses: Lucy, in the 19th century, and Violet in the early 20th century. Today it presents items from different periods in the family's history.

The displays also include items associated with the military careers of members of the family. The small wooden medicine chest in the case by the window was used during the Crimean War by William Herbert, the great-grandfather of the present Earl; it was usual for an officer to take his own medical supplies, as there were few doctors. He left Eton College in the 1850s and went straight to the Crimea.

The portrait to the right of the window shows General Sir Percy Egerton Herbert (1822–76), father of George, 4th Earl. Sir Percy had a distinguished military career, serving in the Kaffir War in 1851–3, the Crimean War (1854–6) and in India (1858–9).

Furniture

Two cabinets on different sides of the room are decorated with 'oyster' veneers, so-called because of their elongated, oyster shapes, achieved by cutting diagonally through the wood. Both were produced in England in the late 17th century.

Tapestries

The two tapestries are part of a set of four depicting the Story of Nebuchadnezzar; the other two are in the Cross Gallery. They were woven in London in the late 17th century.

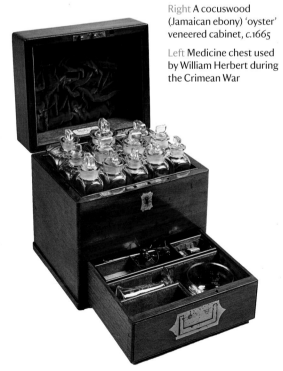

Right A cocuswood (Jamaican ebony) 'oyster' veneered cabinet, c.1665

Left Medicine chest used by William Herbert during the Crimean War

Exquisite illumination

A small showcase in the corner of the room displays a splendid 15th-century Book of Hours, one of the finest examples of an illuminated manuscript in the Trust's care. It was used by Lady Eleanor as an aid to prayer and devotion. She also owned the glass rosary (in the marquetry box on the centre table) that is said to have belonged to Mary Queen of Scots. Evidence suggests that there was a family chapel in the room above, hidden away as their Catholic faith was illegal during the late 16th century.

The State Bedroom

This impressive room was created by William Herbert (who later became the 1st Marquess of Powis) in the 1660s, and had two main purposes. Firstly, it was the last and grandest of the series of rooms that formed the State Apartment; only the most honoured guests would have been invited to enter and see the elaborate decoration. Secondly, it provided a suitably opulent setting for any royal guests who were visiting the castle.

Furniture

Much of the furniture and decoration dates from the late 17th century, although the bed itself was made in about 1780. The bed is slightly raised within an alcove, and is set behind a decorative balustrade, to separate it from the rest of the room. This style was copied from the palace of Versailles, at the time of Louis XIV. It is the only example of this feature still in existence in Britain. The elaborate, high-quality furnishings were possibly also

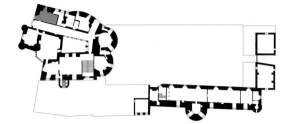

chosen to mimic the style and opulence of the French court. The crimson fabric used for both the bed hangings and the upholstered furniture is English silk cut velvet from *c.*1715.

This room includes some fine furniture with elaborate marquetry: the commode (chest of drawers) with ormolu mounts is French, produced *c.*1690, and the walnut table with floral marquetry is English, from the same period. Elsewhere, the lavish use of gilding on decorative features on the walls and ceiling, together with the silvered gesso sofa, chairs and stools, creates a luxurious effect.

Royal visitors

The future Edward VII stayed here and, in 1909, so did the future George V and Queen Mary. HRH Prince Charles stayed at Powis five times between 1995 and 1999, but chose to sleep in the Duke's Room instead.

The mark of a king

The initials CR are featured in a number of places within the room. The letters probably refer to Charles Rex (King Charles), either Charles I, the martyr king who was executed in 1649, or Charles II, his son who became king when the monarchy was restored in 1660.

Top *Trompe l'oeil* painting from the ceiling in the alcove above the State Bed

Left Marquetry chest with enamel toilet set

The Long Gallery

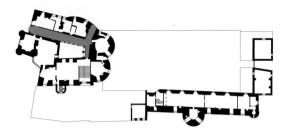

This part of the castle is the only area that remains in the same style as it was in the late 16th century when Sir Edward Herbert lived at Powis. Sir Edward initially leased the castle, but he bought it outright in 1587, and immediately began enriching and improving it. The ornate Elizabethan plasterwork, the chimneypieces and the oak floor were all installed in 1592–4. The wainscot (wooden panelling) was not part of the original scheme, and was probably added in the early 1600s.

Gallery of riches

Today, the Long Gallery presents a combination of late Elizabethan and early Jacobean styles, and displays much of the very fine Baroque sculpture and furniture that was collected by the family. There is a dramatic contrast between the light ceiling and plaster frieze, and the dark floor and *trompe l'oeil* panelling.

Hidden alcove

The gallery has an unusual shape: at the far end it opens to a T shape, with a south-facing window, which creates interesting light patterns. The alcove with the window would originally have been used as a more private area, to which privileged guests might be invited.

Above **The recently restored overmantle in the south window alcove**

Left *Trompe l'oeil* door in the Long Gallery

Plasterwork

The elaborate ceiling plasterwork combines regular curving patterns and flowing foliage, representing the Garden of Eden. Above the fireplace, the plasterwork shows Adam and Eve, with the serpent in the apple tree. The ornate frieze along the walls features mythical beasts and coloured coats of arms, a way of showing the long ancestry of Sir Edward Herbert. The Herbert coat of arms includes a wyvern, a winged creature with the front of a dragon and the scaly tail of a snake.

Indoor exercise

A long gallery was often included in the design of grand homes during the 16th century. It provided an area where the owners and guests might take gentle exercise in inclement weather, enjoy the view of the gardens and estate, and appreciate some of the fine art, particularly family portraits.

Left This overmantle features the arms of Sir Edward Herbert surrounded by plasterwork depictions of Adam and Eve

Above Green man in the plasterwork frieze

Overleaf A long view of the Long Gallery

The Long Gallery, continued

Imperial heads

The Long Gallery displays eight of the full set of Twelve Caesars (Julius Caesar and the first 11 Emperors of Rome); the remaining four are on the ground floor in the Inner Lobby. The busts were produced in Italy in the late 17th century and brought to Powis in 1704; it is the earliest known set surviving in Britain. The heads are made of fine Carrara marble, and the garments and sleeves are made of jasper, Belgian black marble and a number of other marbles.

In the rock

Marble sculpture was much sought after by wealthy art collectors in the 18th century. The four marble putti (cherubs without wings) represent the Four Elements, and are accompanied by the goddess Minerva. These Baroque sculptures were all produced in the early 18th century by Peter van den Branden.

The marble cat was a gift from Robert Clive to his wife, Margaret, who was particularly fond of cats. For many years it was thought to date back to Roman times (1st century BC – 2nd century AD), and was considered particularly unusual because cats were rarely shown in Roman art. Recent research suggests that it may have been made in the 18th century.

Above **Putti representing Earth**, c.1700

Left An 18th-century marble sculpture of a cat

Top table

A large and impressive table stands in the alcove at the far end of the Long Gallery, next to the window overlooking the garden. The *pietre dure* (hard stone) top is made of marble inlaid with lapis lazuli, sardonyx, jasper, agate and other semi-precious stones to create an exquisite pattern of birds and foliage. The table was made *c.*1560 in Italy and is exceptional because it still has its original base: most of the Italian *pietre dure* table tops were exported without the heavy stone bases that supported them. The Powis base is unusual because it is made of gilded wood rather than stone; the use of lions for the supports suggests that the table belonged to a princely family (lions are symbols of power and kings). Family tradition says that the table came from the Borghese Palace in Rome at the end of the 17th century, as a gift from the Pope. This is certainly possible, as the Catholic Herbert family had strong links with Rome at that time.

Above *Pietre dure* table top

Above right The Long Gallery's impressive *pietre dure* table

A narrow escape

In 2007 a major project was carried out to install steel beams under the Long Gallery that would support the immense weight of the eight Caesar busts. These sculptures had been removed from the Long Gallery in the 1950s due to fears that the floor would not carry their great weight: each one weighs about 150kg. The specialist survey (essential before the project could begin) revealed a damaged beam, which clearly would not have supported the weight of the busts. The major structural work carried out will ensure that the Caesars are safe for many years to come.

The State Bathroom
The Walcot Room
The Gallery Bedroom

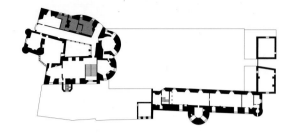

The Gallery Bedroom

The four-poster bed is made of walnut and was produced in Germany in the 1650s. The bed-hangings and curtains are woven Jacquard brocade, made in the early 20th century when Bodley carried out changes to the castle interior. The white marble bust of Napoleon was bought in Paris in 1814 by Edward Herbert (2nd Earl); Napoleon was by then in exile on the island of Elba.

Left **The State Bathroom**

Below **The Walcot Room**

The State Bathroom

This is one of the rooms created in the medieval curtain wall of the castle. When the State Bedroom was set up in the 1660s, this room was probably used as its dressing room. The architect G. F. Bodley transformed it into a bathroom in about 1900.

The Walcot Room

This smaller bedroom was used as a family bedroom, and so lacks the scale and grandeur of the more imposing state rooms. It was named after one of the other homes owned by the Herbert family: Walcot, near Lydbury North in Shropshire. Both the oak bed and the built-in oak wardrobe were probably made by Bodley in the early 20th century; the bed is made from 17th-century carved panels decorated with primitive caryatids (female figures) and Tudor roses.

The Duke's Room
The Lower Tower Bedroom

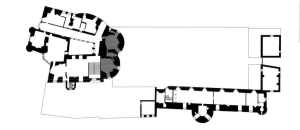

The Duke's Room

This room is named after William, 2nd Marquess of Powis who used it as a bedroom. His father, the 1st Marquess, was very close to James II, who granted William the title of Duke in 1689 as a reward for his loyalty after the Glorious Revolution. The title was not recognised in England by William III or successive monarchs.

The room is one of several that were remodelled in the Jacobean style by Bodley in the early 20th century: the oak panelling was installed in about 1902, and Bodley created two elaborate neo-Jacobean doorcases, only visible from inside the room. The decorative plaster ceiling is late Elizabethan.

Furniture and textiles

The four-poster bed was made c.1600–10, with a heavily carved tester (top frame) and the headboard decorated with caryatids; the bedspread and hangings are hand-embroidered with 17th-century crewelwork. The carpet is unusual as it is hand-worked in cross-stitch, with panels of roses.

The Lower Tower Bedroom

Violet Powis used this as her bedroom in the early 20th century. The mahogany bed with delicate fretwork on the tester was made c.1760. The bedspread is 18th-century Chinoiserie fabric, beautifully embroidered with silver and silver-gilt thread.

Top **The Duke's Room**

Bottom **The Lower Tower Bedroom**

A friendly ghost
Legend tells us that many years ago a sewing woman was working at the castle. A ghostly figure led her to the Duke's Room and indicated something beneath the floorboards. Hidden treasure was revealed, which boosted the Earl's finances.

The Grand Staircase

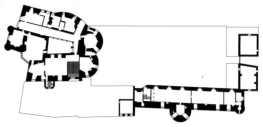

Making an impression

The view of the Grand Staircase from the first-floor landing provides an opportunity to appreciate the scale of the large murals next to the staircase, as well as the ceiling painting above it. In the late 17th century, the Grand Staircase was an essential part of the route for important guests who would be welcomed into the series of impressive rooms known as the State Apartment on the first floor.

Ceiling and wall paintings

The ceiling was painted in the 1670s by the Italian artist Antonio Verrio, who came to England in 1672 and set up a large practice. The painting may represent the apotheosis (raising to the status of a goddess) of Catherine of Braganza, Charles II's queen. Like the Herbert family, she was a Roman Catholic. There is certainly a figure resembling Charles II in the painting, as well as the double 'C' cipher that may represent Charles and Catherine.

The walls on each side of the staircase were painted in 1705 by Gerard Lanscroon, a pupil of Verrio. As you look down the staircase, the painting on the left-hand wall depicts *Venus visiting Vulcan forging the Arms of Aeneas,* and the right-hand wall shows *The Triumph of Neptune and Amphitrite.*

Left **The Grand Staircase**

Unusual items

A long sword hangs on the wall opposite the staircase: this is the late 15th-century broadsword traditionally associated with the Lord President of the Council of Wales and the Marches (a regional administrative and legal body). The Lord President held court at Ludlow Castle between 1478 and 1689, when the Council was abolished after the Glorious Revolution. The 1st Earl's brother-in-law, the Duke of Beaufort, was Lord President between 1672 and 1689.

The large marble statue of a seated Roman figure was put together in the 18th century. The body and head were from different pieces, probably Italian 1st or 2nd century AD; the right arm and left hand are 18th century.

Titles and coronets

Both the ceiling and wall paintings include devices to show the status of William, 1st Earl of Powis, who commissioned the Grand Staircase. The ceiling includes the Powis coat of arms with an earl's coronet above it. The walls were painted after the Earl had been made a Marquess, and also granted the higher-ranking title of Duke by the exiled James II in 1689. The fact that the title of Duke was not recognised by the English monarchy probably irritated the Marquess and his family: the left-hand mural includes his monogram with the coronet of a duke not a marquess, above it!

Above *The large marble statue on the landing*

Left *The Triumph of Neptune and Amphitrite* by Gerard Lanscroon

The Blue Drawing Room

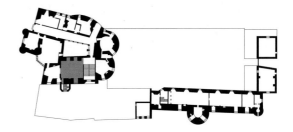

This was one of the suite of rooms that formed the State Apartment in the late 17th century; at that time it would have been used as the Great Chamber or Saloon, the first room to which important guests were escorted. The design of the panelling is very similar to that of the State Bedroom, which suggests a date in the 1660s.

The room has changed little since 1705, when Gerard Lanscroon painted the ceiling, which represents 'Peace Banishing War from the Four Continents' (Europe, Africa, America and Asia – Australia was not then recognised as a continent). In 1752, it was used as a drawing room. The blue and gold colour scheme dates from the 1930s; the gilt sofa and chairs and the large Persian carpet were all brought here in 1937 from the Herbert family's London townhouse in Berkeley Square.

Portraits

To the right of the fireplace is a portrait of Lady Elizabeth Somerset, 1st Marchioness of Powis by John Michael Wright. She and her husband William were both Catholics, loyal to James II. When they accompanied James into exile in France in 1688, William served as Comptroller of the Royal Household and Elizabeth was Governess to the Royal Children.

A large portrait of Mary Preston, 2nd Marchioness, hangs above the fireplace. Mary and her husband William returned from exile in France to reclaim Powis in 1703, and immediately began further improvements to the castle and gardens.

The four pastel miniatures showing the children of Lady Henrietta Herbert and Edward, 2nd Lord Clive, were painted by Anna Tonelli, the children's governess.

Opposite Detail of the late 17th-century Chinese lacquer screen

Below The Blue Drawing Room

Left Miniature portrait of Edward, 2nd Earl of Powis by Anna Tonelli, 1794

Far left Miniature portrait of Lady Charlotte Florentia Clive, later Duchess of Northumberland, by Anna Tonelli, 1794

Tapestries

The three tapestries are from a set of four depicting the story of Julius Caesar: *The Surrender of Cleopatra*, *The Death of Pompey* and *Attack on a Fortress* (the fourth is not on display). They were all produced and signed by Marcus de Vos, one of the principal weavers in Brussels in the late 17th century.

Lovely lacquer

Several pieces of furniture feature oriental lacquer, which became popular in the 17th and 18th centuries. The six-fold screen is Chinese, dating from the late 17th century. The two ornate commodes (sideboards) decorated with Chinese lacquer were made by a French craftsman working in London (Pierre Langlois) in the 1760s. Elaborate commodes like these were for display rather than for use.

On the walls
Large tapestries were often used as portable wall-coverings and draught excluders. They were folded, and sometimes even cut, to fit the space available. This could be one explanation why portions of certain tapestries retain brighter, original colours; some parts have faded less because they were folded back at some point.

The Kitchen
The Billiard Room
The Billiard Room Passage

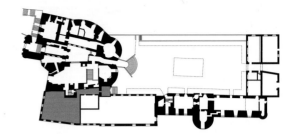

The Kitchen

At the bottom of the staircase descending from the first floor is a door to the right leading to the old Kitchen which was closed after the death of the 4th Countess in 1929. Today it is often used for temporary exhibitions.

The Billiard Room

This was one of the rooms used by the butler, housekeeper and other staff. From 1772 until the 20th century it was the Servants' Hall. The billiard table and the cases of stuffed birds were originally located in the old billiard room (part of the ballroom wing), but were moved here in 1986. Most of the bird collection dates from about 1850. The taxidermy was probably carried out by Henry Shaw of Shrewsbury. Shaw had a good reputation and had many famous clients for his work, including the Dukes of Portland and Westminster.

The Billiard Room Passage

Seven 19th-century oil paintings of prize cattle from the Powis estate hang on the Passage walls. The large, wheeled machine in the corridor is an 18th-century fire engine. This was stored in an out-building, and could have been used to extinguish fires in the castle basement and lower floor with the hoses connected. Opposite the Billiard Room, a door leads from the passage to the cellars, which stored the family's fine wines and large vats of beer for the estate workers and tenants.

Above One of the Powis prize-winning cattle

Left Vats of beer in the cellars

An imposing lead statue stands in the centre of the courtyard: *Fame*, made by Andries Carpentiere. This was originally one of several lead statues in the formal 18th-century water garden on the flat ground beneath the terraces now known as the Great Lawn. The statue was moved here in the late 19th century, after the water garden was dismantled.

The bronze cannon each side of the castle entrance were made *c*.1790 in Seringapatam, India for Tipu Sultan who led the opposition to the British forces in India.

Above The courtyard in 1684 by Thomas Dineley

Left The fire engine

The Ballroom

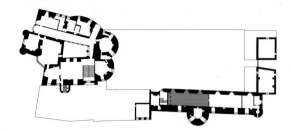

The Ballroom is one of the more recently refurbished parts of the castle. It was commissioned by George Herbert, 2nd Earl of Powis (2nd creation) for the ball to celebrate his 21st birthday in 1776, and includes a minstrels' gallery over the entrance. This area had previously been a long gallery, but it became separated from the main castle by a fire in about 1725.

Edwardian additions

The architect G. F. Bodley carried out some remodelling of the Ballroom in 1902–4. Firstly, he shortened its length, allowing an additional, smaller room to be created at the far end. Secondly, he replaced the 18th-century sash windows with the stone mullions that seemed more appropriate to a castle.

Opposite An embassy to Damascus, detail of the tapestry in the Ballroom

Below The Ballroom

Family books

Today, many of the books collected by the Herbert and Clive families are displayed in the Ballroom. The bookcases were made *c.*1795 of mahogany inlaid with satinwood; they were originally in one of the Herbert family's other homes, Walcot in Shropshire, but were transferred to Powis when Walcot was sold in 1929.

Mysterious piano

The grand piano was made by John Broadwood and Sons, *c.*1854; it was presented to the National Trust by Mr Alec Cobbe in 1983. Like many other properties, Powis has its share of ghost stories. Some people claim to have heard the piano playing in the Ballroom when there is no-one there.

Fine weave

The tapestry is the oldest and most important in the collection. It is dated 1545 and shows an embassy to Damascus, probably based on a contemporary work showing Venetian ambassadors in Damascus. The tapestry came from Lymore, near Chirbury, the home of the Lords Herbert of Chirbury. The Herberts of Powis and of Chirbury were united by marriage in 1751.

Artistic licence

The large picture over the doorway into the Clive Museum is an imaginary representation of the occasion in August 1765 when the Mogul Emperor, Shah Allan II, granted the fiscal administration (or *diwani*) of Bengal, Behar and Orissa to Lord Clive, effectively the foundation of the British Raj in India. The actual event took place in much more mundane surroundings – in Clive's tent with an armchair on the dining table representing the Emperor's throne! This painting by Benjamin West is on long-term loan from the British Library.

The Clive Museum

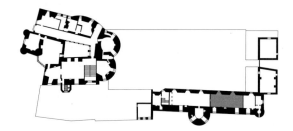

The superb collection of artefacts from India displayed in the Clive Museum is the largest private collection of this type in the UK.

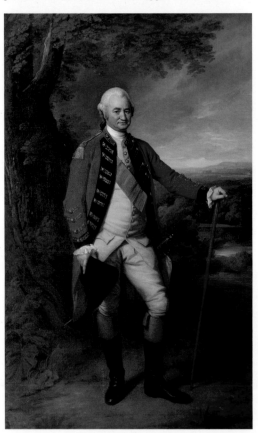

The Clive Museum features over 300 items from India and the Far East, dating from the 17th to the 19th centuries, including ivories, textiles, statues of Hindu gods, ornamental silver and gold, and weapons and ceremonial armour. This impressive collection was created by two generations of the Clive family: Robert (who became known as Clive of India), and his son Edward, who married Henrietta Herbert, daughter of the 1st Earl of Powis (2nd creation).

Robert Clive (1725–74) served in India several times between 1744 and 1767, employed by the East India Company, which promoted trade between India and other countries. There was considerable local unrest and Clive was authorised by the British government to defeat local uprisings; this he did successfully, amassing a personal fortune at the same time.

Left *Robert Clive, 1st Lord Clive* by Nathaniel Dance RA, *c*.1770

Below Detail of silver and partially gilt salver

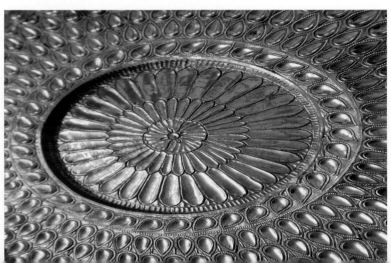

Henrietta Herbert and Edward Clive

The marriage of Henrietta Herbert to Edward Clive in 1784 joined together the two families and provided a sound financial future for Powis. Following in his father's footsteps, Edward was appointed Governor of Madras in 1798. Rather unusually for that time, Henrietta and their two daughters also went to India, and stayed for three years. During this time, Henrietta and Edward collected various Indian artefacts.

In India, the tension between the local population and the British increased in the late 18th century, with the Indian opposition led by Tipu Sultan, the ruler of the south Indian state of Mysore. Events came to a head at the Battle of Seringapatam in 1799. The British forces were led by the Governor General, Lord Mornington, assisted in administrative affairs by Edward, 2nd Lord Clive, Governor of Madras. Tipu Sultan was defeated and many of his possessions were acquired by the British as spoils of war. The spectacular items presented to the Clives included Tipu's magnificent state tent, made of painted chintz; one of the gold tiger's head finials from Tipu's throne; and the two cannon in the courtyard, either side of the castle entrance.

Tiger, tiger

Tipu Sultan was also popularly known as the Tiger of Mysore, hence many of his belongings were decorated with tiger heads. In the Clive Museum, look for the tiger heads on Tipu's sword, the gold finial from his throne and the watercolour showing Tipu seated on his throne.

Top **The Clive Museum**

Above **Ivory Ganjifa playing card**

The Clive Museum, continued

Indian interior

The Clive collection is housed in an area that was originally part of the long, 18th-century Ballroom. In about 1904 G. F. Bodley remodelled the room, shortening it and creating a separate space beyond it, which was used as a Billiard Room until 1952. In 1987, the billiard table was moved to what had been the Servants' Hall in the castle, and the room was set up to display the magnificent collection of Indian artefacts.

The designs of the room and display cases are intended to evoke the architecture and style of India, but within an English setting. This style (known in Britain as Hindu-Gothic) was used for the exterior of Brighton Pavilion, which was built for the Prince Regent (later King George IV) between 1787 and 1823. The display cases were made in 1986–7 by the Sussex cabinet-maker John Hart, to designs by Alec Cobbe.

Amazing artefacts

The Golden Gown was made in the 1950s for the 5th Countess of Powis using 18th-century Indian fabric. It is made of strands of gold laid onto a fabric backing with silk embroidery decoration. A portrait in the State Dining Room shows Lady Powis wearing this gown. Also on display are personal items that belonged to Tipu Sultan, such as his sword, shoes and gloves, as well as one of the gold tiger head finials from his throne. The finial is decorated with diamonds, rubies and emeralds.

The Indian *pan* set is made of silver and partially gilt, with decoration in silver filigree, enamel, foiled glass and turquoise. Such sets were originally used as spice boxes and containers for aromatic leaves which could be offered to visitors to signify the end of a meeting. This one may have belonged to Edward Clive, whose position as Governor of Madras required him to adopt the conventions of Indian ceremonials. It includes a tool for cutting areca nuts.

Over time, the boxes increased in size and decoration, and ladies started to use them to hold treasures and cash.

Above **Silver and enamel *pan* set**

Right **The Golden Gown**

Left **Tipu's gloves**

Opposite **Tipu's gold tiger head**

Tipu's tent
The section of Tipu Sultan's decorated state tent that you can see in the Tent Room (off the Ballroom) is just a small portion: if the whole tent was erected, it would fill the castle courtyard!

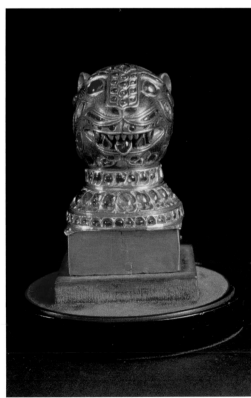

The Coach House and Stables

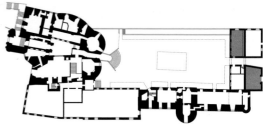

The Coach House and Stables are some of the earliest brick buildings in mid-Wales. They were probably constructed about the same time as the current gateway to the courtyard, replacing parts of the castle that were destroyed when Parliamentary troops seized the castle in 1644 during the Civil War. A keystone over the gateway shows the date 1668.

The displays in the Coach House are unique within the National Trust, as this is the only instance where the collection includes a state coach used for grand ceremonial occasions, the full harness for a pair of horses, and the complete uniforms (liveries) for the coachman and footmen accompanying the coach.

Above left **In the Coach House**

Above right **Carts in the stables**

Opposite **Detail of Sicilian cart**

Below **The State Coach**

The State Coach

The State Coach was built for Edward Herbert, the 3rd Earl of Powis, who inherited the title in 1848. The carriage was used from the family's London home for ceremonial occasions and court functions; the family would have used other carriages for everyday travel.

Violet Powis recorded in her diary when the State Coach was used. On 25 July 1913 she and her husband had attended a dinner at the London home of the Duke of Norfolk to meet the King and Queen: 'We had out the yellow coach – the only time we have had it out for dinner – but I thought it was quite the occasion for it.'

She also described their arrival for a 1914 State Ball at Buckingham Palace, where stringent checks were in place to prevent suffragettes getting in. The Powis coach was recognized by officials and allowed in without being stopped.

All aristocratic families provided a distinctive uniform (livery) for their servants. The coachman wore a white wig and tricorn hat. The two footmen stood at the back of the coach carrying silver-topped canes to look impressive; the canes carried by footmen had originally served a darker purpose – to protect the passengers from attackers! The liveries on display were made in 1898 for staff employed by the 4th Earl of Powis; the coachman, Mills, later became the family's chauffeur.

The harnesses and carriage hammer cloth are decorated with the Earl's crest and coronet in silver plate, rather than the more usual brass. The State Coach was last used in June 2009, for the wedding of Lady Stephanie Herbert, elder daughter of the 8th Earl of Powis.

Carts in the stables

The two carts in the Stables were both used for children. The governess-cart replaced the dogcart around 1900, as it was less likely to tip over. The inward-facing seats also made the cart safer for children to travel in. The brightly decorated Sicilian cart was given to Lady Hermione Herbert in 1905 when she was a girl, and was used at the family's London home, pulled by a donkey.

The Gardens

For many people, the gardens at Powis are one of the highlights of their visit. They are often described as one of the greatest surviving examples of Baroque garden design in Britain.

Below **A riot of colour** on the Orangery Terrace

History of the gardens

Records show that William Herbert, who was made 1st Lord Powis in 1629, had a garden that included some terraces, probably a practical solution to its originally defensive position on irregular land. The 1660s marked the start of major alterations and improvements to the castle to reflect the wealth and increasing status of the Herbert family, and it was natural that these improvements extended to the garden. Work began on additional terraces in the 1680s, probably under the direction of the architect William Winde.

Winde had already created the Grand Staircase at Powis, and was known to take an interest in the gardens of houses he designed. He was also a military engineer and so would have known how to blast terraces out of solid rock.

Unfortunately, improvements to the garden were stopped in 1688 when the 1st Marquess and his family fled to France, accompanying King James II into exile. Work on the garden resumed when the family returned to Powis in 1703, and it seems likely that additional changes to the garden were influenced by the design of the exiled king's court near Paris, at St Germain-en-Laye.

A unique hybrid

At that time, French and Dutch formal gardens were built either on level ground, or as a series of descending wide terraces. However, the site at Powis was not flat, but irregular and hilly. The solution was to have both: formal terraces were carved from the hillside landscape, and a grand water garden was created on the flat land beneath the terraces – a combination that might have been influenced by the design of 16th-century Italian gardens. The water garden included fountains and lead statues: the large statue of *Fame* that stands in the courtyard was originally the centrepiece of the water garden on what is now the Great Lawn. Looking from the terraces to the opposite side of the lawn, there is a grassy slope between the trees – this would have been a water cascade leading down to the water garden.

Ruin and renaissance

By the end of the 18th century, the garden had fallen into neglect, probably a reflection of the family's periods of financial difficulties. In the 19th century, there were some attempts to restore the gardens, with new shrubs, trees and climbers on the terraces. Unfortunately, this was not sustained, and it was only in the early 20th century that a major restoration was fully achieved.

Left The view from the top terrace

Below View of Powis Castle seen across the Great Lawn by Samuel and Nathaniel Buck, 1742

A Perspective View of POWIS CASTLE in the County of Montgomery.

Restoration and beyond

In the early years of the 20th century, the 4th Earl of Powis and his wife Violet carried out major changes. While her husband George worked on renovating the castle with the architect G. F. Bodley, Violet focused on restoring the garden to its former grandeur, recording in her diary her intention to make it 'one of the most beautiful, if not the most beautiful in England and Wales'.

Violet in the garden

Violet's greatest impact was on the formal gardens you can now see to the east of the Great Lawn. This was originally the location of the 18th century kitchen garden, which included glasshouses and brick sheds. After the loss of some large elm trees that had obscured the view of the old kitchen garden, Violet decided to re-locate the kitchen garden behind the Wilderness and create the more

attractive formal garden you see today. She also commissioned the wrought iron gates (from Bodley) to the fountain and sundial garden in 1912 – a present for her husband's birthday.

Today, you can still see many of the elements that have made this a great garden: the dramatic Baroque terraces; the informal woodland opposite; the superb views of surrounding countryside; and the Edwardian formal garden.

Maintaining the gardens

Since 1952, Powis Castle and Gardens have been in the care of the National Trust. The colourful and contemporary-style mixed borders on the terraces are planted to give a long season of interest. At the same time,

Above The Orangery terrace with *Kniphofia* 'Sir C. K. Butler' and *Helenium* 'Sahin's Early Flowerer' in the foreground

Left Gardener using a cherry-picker to clip the massive yew hedging

Eco credentials

Only peat-free compost is used throughout the garden and nursery, and all biodegradable waste is composted. A ground-source heat pump was installed in 2011, and photovoltaic (PV) panels were set up in 2012 to provide some of the energy for the nursery.

Today, the combination of substantial evergreen features, together with luxuriant planting designed to give colour all year round, make Powis a special garden to enjoy at any time of year.

Below Autumn shades at Powis

Bottom Pheasants in the vine arch

they retain the structural elements that are typical of a Baroque garden.

The evergreen yew and box hedges give the garden structure throughout the year, but require annual pruning to maintain their shape. The yew trees on the terraces were originally clipped into formal conical shapes in the 18th century, but today they are 'cloud' pruned from a cherry picker. The serpentine box hedge is cut in June and pruning the yews starts in August. The total time spent clipping the hedges is equivalent to one person working for 46 weeks.

All plant material is either propagated and grown on in the Powis nursery, or is subject to rigorous quarantine measures to ensure no diseased stock can spread plant viruses or bug infestations.

Powis welcomes visitors from all over the world. They are attracted by the superb gardens – the finest Baroque terraced gardens still in existence in Great Britain – and the exceptional quality of the collection displayed in the castle.

Many of the works of art and pieces of furniture are so fine that the amount of sunlight permitted in each room has to be strictly controlled to prevent deterioration. Staff based at the castle, together with experts skilled in conservation techniques, carry out cleaning and restorative work to enable visitors to enjoy the collection to the full – you may see some of this taking place during your visit.

Many pieces displayed in the castle are of such high quality that items are regularly loaned to prestigious museums and art galleries around the world for temporary exhibitions. In recent years, loans have been made to the British Museum, the National Portrait Gallery, the Museum of Fine Art in Houston, Texas and the Musée National des Arts Asiatiques in Paris, as well as to other national and international venues.

Today, staff and volunteers are keen to show visitors a vibrant property. Events throughout the year are designed to bring the property and its history to life for visitors to enjoy. Powis successfully combines a welcoming intimacy with an enthralling grandeur. We hope you share our love of this very special place.

Above A conservator restoring gilding on the base of the *pietre dure* table